D0895904

Kamisama Kiss

9

Story & Art by

Julietta Suzuki

CHARACTERS

Mamoru
Nanami's shikigami.
Nanami Momozono
A high school student who was turned into a kamisama by the tochigami Mikage.
Tomoe
The shinshi who serves Nanami now that she's the new tochigami. Originally a wild fox ayakashi.

Nanami Momozono is a high school student who was evicted from her home when her dad skipped town.
She meets the tochigami Mikage in a park, and he leaves his shrine and his kami powers to her.
Now Nanami spends her days with Tomoe and Mizuki, her shinshi, and with Onikiri and Kotetsu, the onibi-warashi spirits of the shrine.
After holding a festival at her shrine, Nanami starts to really feel her duty as kamisama. She even attends the big kami conference in Izumo, where she manages to fulfill her duties in Mikage's place and deal with the other kamisama.
On the last day of the Kamuhakari, Mikage appears in front of Nanami at the banquet and tells her why he ran away...

Kamisama Kiss

Volume 9
CONTENTS

Chapter 49 005
Chapter 50 038
Chapter 51 069
Chapter 52 099
Chapter 53 131
Chapter 54 161
End Notes 191

護
Kamisama Kiss
Chapter 49

WHAT WERE YOU TALKING ABOUT WITH MIKAGE, NANAMI?
...
NOTHING MUCH.
WE JUST EXCHANGED A FEW WORDS ...
... REALLY?
AYAKASHI LIVE FOR A LONG TIME. THEY LIVE FOR HUNDREDS OF YEARS, CHERISHING ONE LOVE.
TO LOVE AND YEARN FOR SOMEONE ...
...IS THEREFORE A VERY RISKY ACT FOR AN AYAKASHI.

I'M HUMAN ...
...AND WILL DIE BEFORE TOMOE DOES.
SO ISN'T IT SELFISH ...
...FOR ME TO WANT TOMOE?
SOME-THING WRONG, NANAMI?
NO.
THEN WHY DID MIKAGE...
...SAY HE WANTS TOMOE TO CHOOSE ME?

I MAY END UP HURTING TOMOE LIKE HE WAS HURT BEFORE.
YOU LOOK UNHAPPY, NANAMI-HIME.
YOU DON'T HAVE ANYTHING TO DO, SO THERE IS NO NEED TO RUSH HOME.
YOU MAY STAY HERE LONGER IF YOU ARE SAD TO BE LEAVING ME.
WELL, I HAVE SCHOOL ...
IT WAS ONLY FOR SEVEN DAYS, BUT YOU FULFILLED YOUR DUTIES MAGNIFICENTLY.
YOU CAN PROUDLY RETURN TO YOUR SHRINE.

THANK YOU SO MUCH, ÔKUNINUSHI-SAMA.
Yes.
I READ THROUGH THIS "KAMI MONTHLY LIVING" MAGAZINE ...
Fwip
Fwip
YOUR D-
BY THE WAY, NANAMI-HIME.
WHEN SHOULD I PLAN MY DATE WITH THE FEMALE KAMI IN KYOTO?
...AND SHE SEEMS TO BE A VERY NEAT AND PRETTY MAIDEN.
Kayako
I only have one wish. That all people in this world live in peace.
I FIND HER GOALS ADMIRABLE AS WELL.
I WILL BE HAPPY TO GO SEE HER IN PERSON.
...
Kami Monthly Living

KAYAKO IS A WEIRDO BUT SHE'S AN ORDINARY HUMAN GIRL ...
Fwip
GLARE
WHAT ARE YOU SAYING ?
TO ME, FEMALES-KAMI, HUMAN, OR AYAKASHI-ARE ALL LOVEABLE.
THIS IS MY PHILANTHROPY.
KYAH!
I DO NOT CHOOSE!
ÔKUNINUSHI-SAMA, YOU'RE WONDERFUL!
Glomp
...
THEN ...
WHAT ABOUT HUMANS AND YOKAI?
CAN THEY BE UNITED?

IT ALL DEPENDS ON THE ONES IN QUESTION.
IF THEIR LOVE IS THE KIND THAT ENDS IF I SAY "NO" ...
...THEIR LOVE IS NOT THE KIND TO LAST, REGARDLESS.

Sigh
WHAT HAS HAPPENED TO NANAMI-SAMA?
SHE SEEMS DOWN AFTER HAVING ATTENDED THE BANQUET.
SHE MUST BE TIRED.
THE OTHER KAMI ARE STAYING IN IZUMO FOR SEVEN MORE DAYS.
I WANTED NANAMI-CHAN TO RELAX IN THE HOT SPRINGS TOO.
DON'T BE FOOLISH. WE CAN'T LEAVE THE SHRINE UNATTENDED FOREVER.
THEN WHY DON'T YOU RETURN HOME ALONE?
I'LL GO TO THE HOT SPRINGS WITH NANAMI-CHAN—
I'LL STAY HERE WITH NANAMI.
YOU GO HOME.
GRAH
GRAH
THEY'RE FIGHTING AGAIN ...

NANAMI-CHAN, LET'S GO—
WE'RE LEAVING, NANAMI.
GET ON.
BETWEEN ME...
...AND TOMOE...
SORRY ...
...BUT WILL YOU ALL GO HOME FIRST?

THERE'S A PLACE ...
...I WANT TO DROP BY...
...IS A BIG, TALL WALL.
JR
Kyoto
FROM IZUMO TO KYOTO.
I AM SO GLAD YOU TOOK THE TROUBLE TO COME HERE.
SAR-CASM
KAYAKO, LONG TIME NO SEE.
NO WAY.
WHAP
YOU SHOULDN'T HAVE HAD ME COME TO TOWN LIKE THIS!
WE'RE NOT FRIENDS!
HERE'S YOUR SOUVE-NIR.
SO WHY'D YOU COME HERE ?!

I WAS CLOSE BY ...
...SO I WANTED TO SEE YOU.
I WILL GO GREET THE KAMI WHO'S RETURNED FROM IZUMO.
That's what I told them
I DIDN'T LIE.
...
IF YOU HADN'T CALLED ME, I WOULDN'T HAVE BEEN ABLE TO LEAVE ...
...SO IT'S ALL RIGHT.
YOUR BELIEVERS LET YOU LEAVE?
KAYAKO.
YOU'VE CHANGED.
In a good way.
JR
Kyoto

1
Thank you for picking up volume 9 of Kamisama Kiss! I hope you enjoy reading it.
Kamisama Kiss is running in Hana to Yume (on sale in Japan the 5th and 20th of every month).
Kayako
I write a blog, and I post on twitter.
http://suzuju.jugem.jp/
My twitter account is @hiyokosweet
...CHANGED A LITTLE TOO.
YOU'VE ...
SINCE WE'RE IN TOWN ...
WILL YOU COME WITH ME?
I WANT TO HAVE SOME FUN.

ZOMB
ORBIDDEN
I FINISHED 12 LEVELS!
KAYAKO.
BOW
WOO!
RATA TAT TAT
YOU'VE PLAYED THIS GAME A LOT.
I PLAY IT TO WORK OFF STRESS.
PRESS THE CONTINUE BUTTON FAST. YOU'RE NO GOOD AT THIS.
AREN'T YOU WORRIED "KAMI MONTHLY LIVING" WILL CATCH YOU SHOOTING ZOMBIES?
IF THEY DO, I'LL MANAGE.
RATA TAT TAT
B4

Fish Therapy
EEE!
THIS TICKLES.
YOUR FEET GET REALLY SMOOTH.
THE FISH EAT THE DEAD SKIN OFF YOUR FEET.
I WON'T BE ABLE TO DO ANYTHING ...
...IF I'M SCARED OF THE FUTURE AND JUST STAY STILL.
THIS ...
...FEELS STRANGE.

YOU FINALLY SMILED.
DID YOU HAVE A FIGHT ...
YOU SHOULD ALWAYS LAUGH OUT LOUD LIKE THAT.
...WITH YOUR FOX SHINSHI?
SOMEONE IN IZUMO TOLD ME ...
...THAT HUMANS AND AYAKASHI EXPERIENCE THE WEIGHT OF FEELINGS DIFFERENTLY.

AYAKASHI CARRY ONE LOVE WITH THEM FOR-EVER ...
...EVEN AFTER WE'VE DIED ...
WHEN I THOUGHT ABOUT THAT ...
...I KNEW I COULDN'T FORCE MYSELF ON TOMOE ANYMORE.
Hmm
WHAT THE HECK?
YOU'RE SUCH A FOOL.
THAT MEANS THEY'LL NEVER BETRAY YOU.
ISN'T THAT GOOD?
THE TOCHIGAMI IS TIMID ABOUT HER OWN AFFAIRS ...
BY THE WAY ...
...I ...

...IS STRONG-WILLED AS USUAL ...
...BUT ...
N...
...MET KIRIHITO THE OTHER DAY.
KAYAKO...
...I FIND HER ...
...LOVABLE TOO.
NO ...
WHERE?
HOW WAS HE? WAS HE OKAY?
DON'T KNOW.
I MET HIM IN THE LAND OF THE DEAD.
Giggle

WHOMP
WHY WAS HE IN THE LAND OF THE DEAD ?!
TOMOE SAID HE RETURNED SAFELY.
So he's all right.
WHAT THE HECK ?!
...
KIRI-HITO-SAMA ...
...IN THE LAND OF THE DEAD ...
I'LL CALL HIM!
YOU KNOW HIS PHONE NUMBER ?
He's got a phone?
OF COURSE!
HE'S THE ELDEST MOHRI SON. THEY'RE A DIS-TINGUISHED IKEBANA FAMILY.

Snip
Snip
Snip
THAT...
Wah!
Wah!
Wah!
Wah!

...BASTARD FOX.
STAB
I'LL KILL HIM FOR SURE!
KIKU-ICHI!
YES!
LET ME KILL YOU.
I'LL MAKE YOU OVER IN SEVEN DAYS.
K...
K...
KIRI-HITO-SAMA.
!
KIRI-HITO-SAMA.
IS SOME-THING WRONG, KIRI-HITO-SAMA?

NOTHING.
TOMOE.
TOMOE.
TOMOE.
KIRIHITO.

KIRI-HITO ...
ARE YOU THERE?
AFTER HE RETURNED, HE SHUT HIMSELF UP IN HIS ROOM.
NOW HE'S SUDDENLY LEFT.
HE'S LIKE A DIFFERENT PERSON.
I DON'T KNOW WHAT'S GOING ON WITH HIM ...
YES.
YES.
EXCUSE ME.
Bip
NOT TO WORRY.
HE'LL RETURN SOON.

HE'S NOT HOME!
YOU SAID HE'D RETURN SOON.
HUMAN KAMI, WHAT SHOULD I DO?
HE MAY BE IN TROUBLE SOME-WHERE!

CAN'T YOU USE YOUR TSURIKI TO SEE HIM?
I CAN'T. HE'S SHIELDED.
SORRY, HUMAN KAMI, BUT I'M GOING TO KAMAKURA ...

FREEZE
...
OOPS ...
KIRIHITO-SAMA TOLD ME HE DOESN'T NEED ME ANYMORE.
HE SAID "GOOD-BYE" ...

I MAY NOT BE ABLE TO HELP HIM ANY-MORE ...
...BUT ...
...I'M FREE TO CHASE HIM ...
...RIGHT, HUMAN KAMI?

THE LINE OF KAYAKO'S BACK SHOWED NO DOUBTS...
...AND SHE WAS FREE, AS IF SHE HAD WINGS.

KAYAKO!
WAIT...
SHE'LL...
...EASILY FLY OVER THE WALL.
I...
I WANT TO GO WITH HER TOO.

I WANT TO TELL TOMOE...
...THAT I REALLY LIKE HIM.
I WANT TO MOVE FORWARD.
I'll pay for both of us.
Uh, I don't have change.

WE'RE RIDING DIFFERENT TRAINS ...
...SINCE I BOUGHT MY TICKET EARLIER.
I'LL GO NOW, THEN.
OKAY.
WE LIVE EACH MOMENT TO THE FULLEST.
STOP MOPING, AND GET A-HOLD OF YOURSELF.
BUT KIRIHITO-SAMA PROBABLY WON'T SEE ME.
YOU'VE CHANGED, KAYAKO.
In a good way.
YOU CHANGED ME.

1
I HAVEN'T SAID THIS YET ...
...NANAMI.

THANK YOU.
KAYAKO.
I'LL MOVE FORWARD TOO.

EVEN IF I SLAM AGAINST ALL SORTS OF WALLS...

...I WON'T GIVE UP.

I'LL KEEP MOVING.

Kamisama Kiss
Chapter 50

WELL I DO.
AND YOU OWE ME BIIIIG, MOMO-ZONO.

RIGHT!
SATUR-DAY AT 2 P.M. IT IS!
I don't owe you anything.
WH...

WHAT SHOULD I DO?
I'VE NEVER ATTENDED ANYTHING FANCY LIKE A GO-KON ...
...AND I SHOULDN'T BE GOING IN THE FIRST PLACE!
CUZ ...
SOME-THING WRONG, NANAMI?

WE'RE GONNA DO A GO-KON THIS WEEKEND.
YOU TWO ARE GONNA COME TOO ...
...SO GET READY, OKAY?
LIKE A GROUP DATE ?!
I COULDN'T HELP IT. THERE AREN'T ENOUGH GIRLS.
WHY'RE WE GOING TOO?!
I DON'T... WANNA GO ON A GO-KON.
YOU GUYS WANT TO HAVE BOYFRIENDS BEFORE CHRISTMAS, RIGHT?
NOT PAR-TICULARLY ...
THIS IS THE FIRST I'VE HEARD ABOUT IT.

KURAMA AND TOMOE!
TOMOE WAS IN THE HOSPITAL BECAUSE HE WAS SICK?!
THEY'RE ALWAYS SO HANDSOME!
SO HE'S FRAIL ...
WOO!
KURAMA JUST RETURNED FROM OVERSEAS YESTERDAY.
I LOVE HIS UNHEALTHY AURA!
HEY, BOYFRIENDSLESS.
HEY, I GOT A ZERO ON MY ENGLISH VOCABULARY TEST ...
SQUEE SQUEE
Tomoe?
I'VE GOTTA RECORD KURAMA IN WARATTE IIKAMO ...

Gloom
The ceremonies at Izumo are over and Nanami has finally returned home.
Her dazzling but peaceful everyday-life has resumed.
EEK, LOOK!
IT'S BEEN A WHILE SINCE THEY'VE BEEN TO SCHOOL!

I'M ALREADY IN LOVE WITH A FOX.
THAT LOOKED LIKE AN INTENSE CONVERSATION.
N...
NOT AT ALL.
Stretch
I...
IT'S NOTHING.
YOU SAID YOU WERE GOING ON A GO-SOME-THING!
DON'T LIE.

...SO I CAN AVOID UN-NECESSARY MISUNDER-STAND-INGS.
Stomp
Let's go home
Stomp
A GUY SHOULDN'T BUTT IN ON GIRLS' TALK.
I WON'T TELL HIM ...
Whap
WE'RE JUST GOING OUT FOR SOME FUN!
CUZ I...
...ONLY LIKE TOMOE.
...
SHE FLATLY REJECTED YOU, FOX.

I TOLD YOU IT'S DIFFICULT DEALING WITH HUMANS.
ESPECIALLY GIRLS NANAMI'S AGE.
NANAMI SAID IT WAS NOTHING.
YOU'RE SO SURE.
DO YOU REALLY BELIEVE NANAMI WON'T GO ANYWHERE?
Fwoosh
Gyah!
BESIDES.

...I DON'T WANT HIM TO DOUBT MY FEELINGS FOR HIM.
How do you do?
We're girls from Ujigami High.
I'M YAMADA.
SATO.
TANAKA.
KOHIRUMAKI. NICE TO MEET YOU.
THAT'S IT FOR INTRODUCTIONS.
YOU'RE CUTE.
SO EVERY-ONE'S A TEEN-AGER? YOU'RE YOUNG.
BOYS MUST LOVE YOU AT SCHOOL.
NOOOO.

SO.
DOES ANYONE HAVE A BOYFRIEND ALREADY?
STUPID, DON'T ASK THAT QUES-TION.
EVEN IF THEY DID, THEY WOULDN'T ADMIT IT.
THEY WOULDN'T BE HERE IF THEY DID.
Right?
WHY? I'VE GOT A GIRL-FRIEND BUT I SHOWED UP.
I SHOULDN'T HAVE?
UM.
KILL...
SHUT UP, YOU FOOL.
DIE.
SO.
LET'S ORDER SOME DRINKS.
Ha ha ha I want a Beer!
A 104
A 103
SO...
AS FAR AS I CAN TELL ...

THE ROOM NEXT DOOR.
...IT'S JUST A GO-KON.
夜
A GO-KON?
WHAT'S A GO-KON?
TOMOE-KUN, YOU DON'T EVEN KNOW WHAT A GO-KON IS, BUT YOU'RE SITTING HERE LOOKING LIKE A CASANOVA?
I'M SO EMBARRASSED I'M BLUSHING.

A GO-KON IS WHERE HORNY MEN AND WOMEN WHO'RE MEETING FOR THE FIRST TIME GET TOGETHER TO COMMIT LECHEROUS ACTS. RIGHT, TENGU?
NO. SHUT UP.
WHAT SORT OF DISREPUTABLE EVENT WOULD THAT BE?
SO WHY IS NANAMI AT SUCH AN EVENT?!
Dunno.
SHE PROBABLY JUST WANTED TO HAVE SOME FUN.
SHE'S A TEEN-AGER.
...
SHE DOESN'T LIVE AROUND HUMANS, SO SHE PROBABLY WANTS TO HAVE FUN WITH HER OWN KIND.
TWITCH
MMM!
THIS IS GOOD.

RIGHT?
THE FOOD HERE IS PRETTY GOOD.
THIS IS THE FIRST TIME I'VE COME TO A PLACE LIKE THIS.
YOU'VE NEVER COME TO SING KARAOKE?
NO.
SHE'S GOT A BROKEN HEART AND IS LOOKING FOR A BOY-FRIEND.
I'M NOT LOOKING FOR ONE!
EEK!
ZOOO
IN MY BAG!
BOING
THERE'S A SNAKE!
SPARKLE

MIZUKI ?!
W.C
?
WHY'RE YOU HERE ?!
IN THE BATH-ROOM
I WANTED TO JOIN YOU CUZ YOU'RE ALWAYS HAVING FUN IN PLACES ...
...I'VE NEVER BEEN BEFORE.
DID YOU COME HERE ALONE ?!
NO.
IS...
...TOMOE HERE TOO?
Grab
SORRY, SORRY.

WHA...?
WHA...?
WHY'RE YOU HERE ?!
Wah
Wah
Wah
YOU WERE ACTING STRANGE, SO I WAS WORRIED AND FOLLOWED YOU.
S...
SO HE SAW ME?!
BUT ...
...THERE WAS NO NEED FOR ME TO WORRY.
MY LOVELY MIZUKI BOTHERED YOU WHEN I LOOKED AWAY.
TOMOE.

YOU HAD A DIFFICULT TIME IN IZUMO.
NOT TO WORRY. WE SHALL LEAVE ...
...SO FEEL FREE TO ENJOY YOUR-SELF.

AH.
I SEE.
TOMOE DOESN'T CARE...
NANAMI ?
...BUT I WAS ABOUT TO TRY TO JUSTIFY MYSELF...
SOME-THING WRONG ?
I'M NOT DOING ANYTHING WRONG ...
...IF I'M HAVING FUN WITH GUYS HE DOESN'T KNOW.
I'M A FOOL.

NOT AT ALL ...
A 145
GLOOM
I'M SUCH A FOOL ...
I'M ...
...FINE. REALLY.
I JUST REMEMBERED THE TIME I GOT REJECTED.
Ha Ha Ha
THAT'S HAPPENED TO ME TOO.
MAYBE THE GO-KON WORE YOU OUT.
LET'S COOL DOWN IN THE NIGHT BREEZE.

THANK YOU.
AND THANKS FOR LENDING ME YOUR COAT.
Ha Ha Ha
NO PROB-LEM.
BUT WHY?
YOU'RE REALLY NICE.
I WAS A LITTLE WARY OF YOU AT FIRST.
I THOUGHT YOU WERE CUTE FROM THE START.
HMM ?
YOUR HAND ...
HMM ?
Squeeze
...IS SOFT.

KICK
CAN I HOLD—
WHO THE HELL ARE YOU ...?
WHA ...?
SORRY, SORRY.

Kara
I-I'LL GO BACK FIRST.
Tmp
Tmp
...
I THOUGHT YOU WENT HOME ...
...TOMOE ...
SHEESH.
MY LOVELY MIZUKI ...
...SEEMS TO HAVE BOTHERED YOU.

2

Bonjour! Kumamoto

I took the new bullet train "Sakura" and went to Kumamoto, the country of fire.

I met Mizuho Kusanagi Sensei, creator of *Akatsuki no Yona*! I got her autograph too.

I listened to her talk a lot about manga. It was so fun!

Kumamoto castle has become very clean! The station changed since my last visit and I was surprised! I'd like to take the new bullet train and visit again.

WHY DID HE HAVE TO SHOW UP NOW?

...LIKE I WAS FLIRTING WITH THAT GUY.

IT LOOKED...

I SAID ENJOY YOURSELF ...

...BUT I DIDN'T SAY YOU COULD MAKE OUT WITH A WEAKLING LIKE HIM.

I...

I WAS DOING NO SUCH THING. HOW COULD YOU!

IT WAS ...

"DO YOU
REALLY
BELIEVE
...

... "NANAMI WON'T GO ANYWHERE?"
LET'S GO.
WHA?
HEY WAIT, I CAN'T JUST LEAVE EVERYONE BEHIND AND GO HOME!
Tmp
I HAVE OUR VEHICLE READY AT A NEARBY PARK.
TODAY'S A HOLIDAY, SO THE BUSES STOP RUNNING EARLY.
I ALREADY TOLD THEM YOU'RE LEAVING.
WHA ?!
Tmp
Tmp
Tmp
Tmp
MY ARM HURTS.

I CAN'T SHAKE HIM FREE.
TOMOE ...
ARE YOU...
...FEELING CRANKY?

YANK
YOU'RE IN A BAD MOOD ...
I WAS RIGHT.
...CUZ I WAS WITH A BOY.
HEH HEH.

WAIT!

Heh Heh
DON'T SAY ANY-THING!
IT'S SO FUNNY, I'M GONNA PRETEND IT'S TRUE!
...
BUT I CAN'T JUST LEAVE LIKE THIS.
I'LL GO TELL EVERYONE I'M GOING HOME.
I need to return this coat, too.
SO TOMOE, YOU GO FIRST—
YOU'RE RIGHT.
I'M UPSET.
I'M ACTING LIKE A CHILD.
TOMOE
...

I GUESS I'M NOT AS GROWNUP ...
...AS EVERYONE THINKS I AM.
...LOOKED ANXIOUS AS HE TURNED AWAY...
...BUT IS THAT BECAUSE THAT'S HOW I WANT HIM TO FEEL?

GRAB
OR...
OR ...
D—

HOW LONG HAVE YOU BEEN HERE ?!
HOW LONG ?
The whole time.
...
THUMP THUMP
DOES HE LIKE ME?
Meanwhile, Kurama ...
...was enjoying being onstage.

Kamisama Kiss
Chapter 51
The Mohri residence, Kamakura.

SOMEONE NAMED YATORI WANTS TO SEE ME.
YATORI ...
DON'T KNOW HIM.
SO AFTER KAYAKO COMES A LOW-LEVEL YOKAI?
PEOPLE DON'T RESPECT ME LIKE THEY USED TO.
SHFF
I FIND IT ANNOYING THAT HE SENT KIRI-HITO-SAMA A LETTER LIKE THIS.
I SHALL GO FIND OUT WHO HE REALLY IS.
LEAVE HIM ALONE.
WE DON'T HAVE TIME TO WASTE ON SMALL-TIME YOKAI.
KIRI-HITO-SAMA.
MAY I EAT THE SWEETS THAT THE HUMAN KAMI GAVE US?
...
GO AHEAD.
YAY!

WHOA, THESE LOOK DELICIOUS.
I WOULD LOVE TO HAVE ONE.
WHAM
EEK!
GRR
RR
WHO ARE YOU?
Uh...
AH!
SKKKKSH
NOOOOO!
F-F-F-FORGIVE ME.
I'M ASKING WHO YOU ARE.
R-RIGHT.

I AM YATORI.
WOOP
PLEASE ALLOW ME ...
...TO HELP BRING AKURA-OH-SAMA'S BODY BACK FROM THE LAND OF THE DEAD.
I CAME HERE BECAUSE I HEARD YOU ARE TRYING TO RESURRECT AKURA-OH-SAMA, WHO IS SLEEPING IN THE LAND OF THE DEAD.
...

YOU?
WHY?
AKURA-OH-SAMA WILL BRING ABOUT MY IDEAL WORLD!
HE DESERVES TO RULE!
I AM DOING THIS OUT OF DEVOTION TO HIM!
I FIND THAT COMFORTING...
...BUT CAN YOU DO IT?
SO HE DOESN'T REALIZE I AM AKURA-OH.
WHAT A FOOL.
HIS EYES CANNOT PERCEIVE MY EMOTIONS...
PROVE TO ME...
...THAT YOU AREN'T ALL TALK.
...YET HE MENTIONS DEVOTION.
I understand that you might doubt me.
OF COURSE...
...I HAVE MY PLANS READY!

I SHALL MAKE THE TENGU OF KURAMA MINE ...
...AND SERVE YOU WITH AN ARMY!
I WILL OFFER THE SACRED MOUNT KURAMA TO AKURA-OH-SAMA AS PROOF OF MY LOYALTY.
I CANNOT TRUST...
I LOOK FORWARD TO HEARING GOOD NEWS, YATORI.
...A YOKAI LIKE HIM ...
...BUT I WILL USE WHAT I CAN.
YES ...

...I SHALL NOT DISAPPOINT YOU.
THEY WERE NICE.
THEY GAVE ME SOME SWEETS.
DO NOT BE FOOLED. I COULD TELL RIGHT AWAY ...
...THAT HE IS AKURA-OH, ALTHOUGH HE IS PRETENDING TO BE HUMAN.
HE TURNED HIS BACK ON US SO EASILY.
AKURA-OH HAS FALLEN LOW.
...AND NICE PEOPLE CANNOT LIVE LONG.
PEOPLE SAY THE DEVIL LOOKS AFTER HIS OWN ...

Fidget
Fidget
...I FORGOT TO ASK ...
YESTER-DAY ...
Hmm.
YOU'VE GOT RICE ON YOUR FACE, NANAMI.
...BUT DO YOU ...
THERE'S NONE ON ME!
WHERE'S THE RICE?!
Glare
YOU'RE TOO YOUNG TO BE GOING OUT AT NIGHT.
WELL, WELL. YOU'RE A SLOPPY WOMAN.
?!
!!!

Next time, next time.
Uh, I hope there's a next time.
Mumble
I SHOULD'VE ASKED HIM YESTER-DAY!
LET'S GO HOME.
NANAMI'S LESSON FOR TODAY:
AN OPPORTUNITY MISSED IS AN OPPORTUNITY LOST.
TROMMP
DID YOU STEP ON ME, WOMAN ?!
HOW DARE YOU!
I'M SORRY, I DIDN'T THINK SOME-BODY WAS SLEEPING HERE ...
GLARE
GNH.

HE'S A TENGU ?!
I WASN'T ASLEEP. I HAD MY EAR TO THE GROUND.
I AM BOTANMARU OF MOUNT KURAMA!
WHAT'S A LITTLE TENGU DOING IN THE HUMAN WORLD?
You're cute! ♡
I HAVE COME TO LOOK FOR SOME-ONE!
I AM LOOKING FOR SHINJURO-SAMA, LEGITIMATE SON OF THE THIRD SOJOBO-SAMA!
BAM
Shinjuro-sama should look like this now
HE MUST HAVE GROWN TO BE A FINE TENGU LIKE THIS!
He should have
Grr
DON'T YOU KNOW WHERE HE IS ?!
He doesn't look cute at all.
Not at all.
Shinjuro-sama
17 years ago
HE VANISHED TO THE HUMAN WORLD 17 YEARS AGO, AND IS MISSING.

TOMOE ...
HEY!
Ah!
HURL
GO TO MOUNT TAKAO AND ASK YOUR COMRADES.
NO.
I WILL NOT FORGIVE YOU, FOX YOKAI!
HOW DARE YOU!
Sorry he's such a violent fox
ARE YOU ALL RIGHT? YOU'RE NOT HURT?
SPLAT
...
YOU CAN'T FLY.
SO...

WAIT!
LEAVE HIM ALONE.
NO!
Whap
I CAN'T LEAVE HIM ALONE!
TOMOE, YOU GO HOME FIRST!
Take care of Mamoru

BOTAN-MARU.
MAY I HELP LOOK FOR SHINJURO?
TELL ME MORE ABOUT HIM.
BOTAN-MARU.
BOTAN-MARU.

ARE YOU CRYING AGAIN, BOTANMARU?
DID JIRO STRIKE YOU AGAIN?
COME, SHOW ME.
BIG BROTHER.
I HATE MYSELF.
A TENGU BORN LAST YEAR IS TALLER THAN ME NOW.
I'M ALREADY SIX ...
...YET MY WINGS HAVEN'T COMPLETELY GROWN.
SHIN-JURO?
SHINJURO WAS LIKE YOU TOO.
HE WAS BORN THE SON OF THE THIRD SOJOBO...BUT IT TOOK TIME FOR HIS BODY TO FULLY MATURE...

JIRO OFTEN STRUCK HIM.
...AND THE OTHER TENGU TREATED HIM HARSHLY.
HE WAS THE FIRST CHILD BORN IN 500 YEARS ...
BUT ...
...HE DID NOT CRY.
THE ROCK WHERE YOU'RE SITTING NOW.
HE ALWAYS SAT ON THAT ROCK.

BE STRONG, BOTANMARU.
WHERE IS SHINJURO-SAMA NOW?
I DO NOT KNOW. HE WAS TERRIBLY HURT WHEN HE WAS 12 ...
...AND LEFT THIS MOUNTAIN. HE'S BEEN MISSING SINCE.
WE DO NOT WANT TO LOSE YOU AS WELL ...
PEOPLE SAY TENGU WHO LEAVE THE MOUNTAIN ARE DROPOUTS.
BUT I DON'T BELIEVE IT.
I AM SEVEN, BUT I CANNOT EVEN FLY.
TENGU BECOME ADULTS IN EIGHT YEARS. BUT VERY RARELY, SOMEONE SLOW TO MATURE LIKE ME IS BORN.

3
My pets
VIVI
MIYA
MOANA
SAKURA
CIRO
I WOULD LIKE TO SEE SHINJURO-SAMA AND TALK TO HIM.
IF I'M ABLE TO SEE SHINJURO-SAMA, WHO HAS GROWN TO BE A FINE TENGU ...
...I ...
...I ...
SOB
SOB
WHAT IS IT ?!
YOU'RE ONLY SEVEN ...
...BUT YOU'VE GONE THROUGH A LOT!
I'm sorry! I called you cute!
WOM
LET US ...
...GO LOOK FOR SHINJURO!

HE MUST BE A FINE MAN NOW FOR SURE.
SOMEONE YOU'LL LOVE.
Of course
SHIN-JURO-SAMA!
FOUND HIM.

Melody Kiss
KURAMA
SO KURAMA...
N...
NO!
I'M SURE THAT'S HIM! HE LOOKS EXACTLY LIKE THE PORTRAIT IN THE TREASURY!

WHY'D YOU SUDDENLY WANT TO SEE ME?
...IS SHINJURO ?!
KURAMA
IF YOU'D TOLD ME TWO MONTHS AGO, I'D HAVE HAD THE WHOLE NIGHT FREE FOR YOU.
SUPER SUPER
DID YOU SEE MY NEW TV COMMERCIAL AND COULDN'T HELP BUT COME TO ME?
I'M OVER-WHELMED THAT A FEMALE KAMI WANTS THIS FALLEN ANGEL.

I DIDN'T COME TO SEE YOU.

Pant Wheeze
Pant Wheeze
...
TOO BAD, BUT I'M ALL BOOKED.
YOU CAN TALK TO ME AT SCHOOL.

BUT I BROUGHT SOMEONE ...
...WHO DID.
BOTAN-MARU.
HINJURO-SAMA!

WHO'S THAT BRAT?!
HE'S BOTANMARU.
Panic
Panic
I AM VERY HAPPY I WAS ABLE TO MEET SHINJURO-SAMA...
I AM BOTANMARU OF MOUNT KURAMA!
...ON THIS AUSPISUS... AUSPISIS.
...day
DARN...
I CAN'T SPEAK PROPERLY!
AND SHINJURO-SAMA IS RIGHT IN FRONT OF ME!
YOU'RE...

...SMALL. HOW OLD ARE YOU?
I...
I AM SEVEN.
SHINJURO-SAMA...
WHAT BIG HANDS HE HAS ...
SHINJURO ...

I DON'T KNOW WHY YOU'RE HERE ...
...BUT YOU SHOULD RETURN RIGHT NOW.
I WANT TO BE LIKE HIM.
I CAN DO IT.
...WAS LIKE YOU TOO, BOTANMARU ...
I WOULD LIKE TO BECOME LIKE SHINJURO-SAMA.
A CHILD TENGU IS FORBIDDEN TO LEAVE THE MOUNTAIN.
YOU MUST'VE LEFT WITHOUT TELLING ANYONE.
I CAN'T TAKE CARE OF A RUNAWAY ...
...SO GO HOME.
WHA ...?
NO.
I...

...HAVE COME TO GET YOU ...
...SHINJURO-SAMA.
OUR MOUNTAIN IS IN SERIOUS TROUBLE ...
THE MOUNTAIN HAS BEEN COVERED IN CLOUDS OF MIASMA SINCE SOJOBO-SAMA COLLAPSED.
JIRO-SAMA WAS ELECTED SUCCESSOR ...
...BUT MANY OPPOSE THAT DECISION ...
...AND WE ARE ALL SPENDING OUR DAYS IN FEAR.
IF SHINJURO-SAMA RETURNS ...

...
WHAT CAN I DO ...
...BOTAN-MARU?

YOU KNOW I LEFT THE MOUNTAIN 17 YEARS AGO.
I'M A DROPOUT.

Ouch.
NO!

I'll never return to the mountain, cuz there're only guys there.
I'M TOTALLY ATTACHED TO THE HUMAN WORLD NOW ...
...CUZ THERE'RE SO MANY CUTE GIRLS HERE.

SHIN-JURO-SAMA IS NOT A DROPOUT!
I AM AIMING ...
...TO BECOME LIKE SHINJURO-SAMA!

HEY!
Grab
BOTAN-MARU ?!
ARE YOU ALL RIGHT?! WHAT'S WRONG WITH YOU?
HE'S ALL RIGHT.
HE SHOULDN'T HAVE LEFT THE MOUNTAIN WHEN HE WAS STILL A KID.
THAT IS WHY I WANT YOU TO STAND AS OUR LEADER.
YOU...
...AND I ARE THE SAME.

A CHILD TENGU IS RAISED BY THE MOUNTAIN ITSELF.
THAT'S WHY A TENGU SHOULDN'T DESCEND TO THE HUMAN WORLD WHILE HE'S STILL A CHILD.
HE'S INHALED TOO MUCH OF THE POISON OF THE HUMAN WORLD.
JIRO-SAMA WAS ELECTED AS SUCCESSOR ...

WH-WHAT IS THIS? YOU'RE HURT.
Botanmaru!
HE WAS WHIPPED.
DAMN ...
I DIDN'T THINK I'D HAVE TO RETURN SO SOON.

Kamisama Kiss
Chapter 52

IS BEING SOJOBO'S SON A GOOD THING?
NO.
SHINJURO, YOU STILL CAN'T FLY BY YOURSELF?
YOU'RE ALREADY FIVE. YOU'RE THE ONLY ONE RIDING A CROW.
YOU'RE SOJOBO-SAMA'S CHILD, BUT YOU'RE NO GOOD.
THE ONLY THING GOOD ABOUT YOU IS THE KIMONO YOU'RE WEARING.
TO ME, BEING SOJOBO'S SON IS ONLY A BURDEN.
AND MY BIG BROTHERS TAUNT ME ABOUT IT.

Pout
WHY HAVEN'T YOU CHANGED?
ARE YOU GOING TO ATTEND THE CEREMONY WEARING THAT KIMONO?
YES.
I WILL WEAR WHAT EVERYONE ELSE IS WEARING.
I AM INFERIOR TO THEM, SO I SHOULDN'T WEAR A KIMONO THAT'S BETTER THAN THEIRS.
OTHERWISE I'LL BE A CLOWN.
Whap
THIS IS TRADITION.
SHINJURO.
...
DO NOT COMPLAIN ABOUT YOUR KIMONO.
ENOUGH.
YOUR ROOM, YOUR FOOD!
DO YOU THINK THOSE ARE LIKE EVERYONE ELSE'S?
SOJOBO'S CHILD SHOULD NOT BE SO SELFISH.

I WAS SMALL, AND DIDN'T REALIZE HOW ALONE I WAS.
I NEVER THOUGHT BEING ALONE WAS LONELY.
I WILL SLEEP WITH EVERYONE ELSE STARTING TONIGHT.
BAM
Bow
PLEASE LET ME STAY HERE.
I'VE HARDLY TALKED TO MY FATHER.
I'VE ONLY MET HIM A FEW TIMES.
HE HAD A BUSHY BEARD.
AM I GOING TO BE LIKE HIM?

MY FUTON IS GONE!
I put it right here.
HEH HEH HEH
SO IT WAS YOUR FUTON.
I THREW IT AWAY CUZ IT SMELLED LIKE MILK.
Hee Hee Hee
WHY DON'T YOU GO BACK TO YOUR ROOM AND SLEEP ON A TATAMI MAT?
DAMMIT...
HA HA HA
COME, SHINJURO.
YOU CAN SLEEP IN MY FUTON.

...I
...
...NEVER KNEW THE WARMTH OF ANOTHER BODY.
UNTIL I MET BROTHER SUIRO...

LISTEN ...
I'M SIMPLY TAKING BOTANMARU HOME AND SEEING HOW MY FATHER IS DOING.
NOTHING AMUSING WILL HAPPEN, SO YOU DON'T NEED TO COME WITH ME.
WE AREN'T COMING TO FOOL AROUND!
WE'RE COMING TO ASSIST YOU!
YOU'RE GOING BACK TO HELP THE FAMILY YOU RAN AWAY FROM.
I BROUGHT LOTS OF WHITE OFUDA, SO I CAN HELP!
FWOOSH

I NEVER KNEW YOU WERE SOJOBO'S SON.
YOU'RE SUCH AN ORDINARY TENGU, I'D NEVER HAVE GUESSED THE TRUTH.
AND WHY'S THE FOX HERE? I DIDN'T INVITE HIM.
I ENJOY OBSERVING OTHERS GET INTO TROUBLE.
HEH, REALLY?
I ASSUMED ...
YOU TWO! IF YOU WANNA FIGHT, DO IT AFTER WE'RE THERE.
Ah Geez
Gyan
Gyan
CUZ THE FOX CAN BE SO JEALOUS.
...YOU RUSHED OVER CUZ YOU DIDN'T WANT NANAMI AND ME BEING ALONE TOGETHER.
BOTAN-MARU IS STILL ASLEEP.
MMM ...
WHERE AM I?

YOU AWAKE, BOTAN-MARU?
WHAT HAP-PENED TO ME?
YOU COLLAPSED CUZ YOU WERE SO TIRED.
I GAVE YOU SOME MOMOTAN, SO YOUR WOUNDS ARE ALL HEALED TOO.
HOW?
YOU ARE RIGHT.
MOMOTAN IS KAMI MEDICINE. IT HEALS ANY WOUND OR ILLNESS.
I DON'T KNOW WHY SOJOBO COLLAPSED ...
...BUT HE MAY RECOVER IF HE TAKES SOME MOMOTAN.
IS THAT TRUE, FOX?
RAH
YOU DARE CALL ME A FOX, YOU BRAT?

Grab
OOPS.
THE FOX WILL BITE IF YOU GET TOO CLOSE ...
...CUZ HE'S BURNING WITH JEALOUSY.
SO, HOW DID YOU MANAGE TO TRAVEL WHEN YOU CAN'T EVEN FLY?
I-I DE-SCENDED THE MOUNTAIN ON A CROW.
WHEN I TOLD BROTHER SUIRO I WANTED TO COME GET SHINJURO-SAMA ...

SOMETHING WRONG, SHINJURO-SAMA?
...HE LENT ME A CROW.
NO.

The humans see Mount Kurama as merely a mountain ...
...but the tengu live in the hidden Mount Kurama.
AND THE ENTRANCE TO IT ...
...IS SOJOGADANI VALLEY.
SO YOUR HOME IS IN THE MOUNTAINS. IT REMINDS ME OF SCHOOL TRIPS.
The air tastes good.
YOU LIVE IN THE MOUNTAINS TOO.
I live in a big city.
MMM, NEGATIVE IONS.
REFRESHING.
WATCH OUT, TOCHIGAMI.
THIS FORKED CEDAR TREE IS THE ENTRANCE TO OUR MOUNTAIN ...
...AND WE'LL BE ENTERING IT NOW.

YOU'RE RIGHT.
THE AIR'S SUDDENLY DIFFER-ENT.
IT'S DARK EVEN THOUGH IT'S MORNING ...
THERE'S SOME FOG.
STAY WITH ME, NANAMI.
Grr
THE PLANES OF EXISTENCE CAN BECOME WARPED IN A MOUNTAIN WITH THICK MIASMA.
IF YOU GET LOST, YOU WON'T BE ABLE TO RETURN.

THIS MIASMA IS TERRIBLE ...
YES... IMPURITIES GREW THICK AFTER SOJOBO-SAMA'S AURA WANED.
HOW-EVER.
THINGS WILL RETURN TO NORMAL WHEN SOJOBO-SAMA RECOVERS!
B...
BUT SOMEDAY ...

...I WOULD LIKE SHINJURO-SAMA ...
...TO BE THE FOURTH SOJOBO-SAMA!
BROTHER SUIRO.
I'D LIKE YOU TO BECOME THE FOURTH SOJOBO.
FATHER HAS A BUSHY BEARD AND LOOKS GRIM, BUT YOU ARE HANDSOME.
THE TENGU OF ATAGO AND TAKAO WILL ALL ENVY US.

I AM SERIOUS.
YOU HAVE THE FASTEST WINGS ON THE MOUNTAIN, AND YOU PLAY THE FLUTE VERY WELL.
PLAY MY FAVORITE UZUZAKURA SONG AGAIN.
ME, THE FOURTH SOJOBO?
WHAT A FUNNY THING TO SAY, SHINJURO.
GRAB
SHIN-JURO ...
...YOU SOUND CON-GESTED.
IT'S ALL RIGHT.
HAVE YOU BEEN CRYING? DID JIRO STRIKE YOU AGAIN?
HE KEEPS HITTING YOU WHEN I'M NOT AROUND ...
IT'S MY FAULT I'M WEAK.
BROTHER JIRO IS ONLY A LITTLE HARSH.

THEN ...
...I SHALL PLAY A PIECE FOR YOU.
THE UZUZAKURA SONG THAT YOU LOVE.
SUIRO.
I WAS SO PROUD OF YOU.
YET ...
...BE-CAUSE OF ME ...

4
I went to Mount Kurama because I'm doing a story about tengu.
I've been saying since volume 3 that I've got to draw about Kurama, and I was finally able to.
This was my second time climbing Mount Kurama, and my legs were so tired. I need to exercise more.
I saw a man in a suit climbing while carrying a suitcase.
I saw a woman climbing in high heels!
Amazing.
BROTHER SUIRO!
SHIN-JURO-SAMA ?!

I'M ALL RIGHT.
I'VE COME ALL THE WAY HERE...
WHAT IS WRONG. ARE YOU FEELING ILL?
WAIT, BOTAN-MARU.
YES?
...YET I'M FEELING SCARED NOW?!
DAMMIT...!
NANAMI AND TOMOE ARE GONE ...
THE FOG IS GETTING EVEN THICKER.
YOU ALL RIGHT, NANAMI?
NO...

SHIN-JURO-SAMA!
THIS FOG IS ...
FLAP
THIS ISN'T AN ORDINARY FOG. THIS ...
...IS A BARRIER.
SO WE'RE TRAPPED INSIDE IT.

...GET HIM BACK HOME ...
BUT I'VE GOT TO ...
BOTAN-MARU!
WE'RE TURNING BACK. THIS FOG ...
...IS A BARRIER ...

THIS IS TO KEEP US OUT.

WELL OF COURSE THEY WOULDN'T WELCOME US ...

AND YOU RAN AWAY FROM THE MOUNTAIN AS SOON AS YOUR WOUNDS WERE HEALED.
FORGIVE ME, BROTHER SUIRO ...
I...
YOU DO NOT NEED TO APOLOGIZE, SHINJURO.
IF YOU DIE ...
...THE FOG IN MY HEART WILL LIFT A LITTLE.
I SHOULD HAVE IGNORED YOU.
I SHOULDN'T HAVE CARED ABOUT YOU.

NO, BROTHER JIRO!
I SHALL TRAIN YOU!
COME, SHIN-JURO!
YOU'RE ALREADY TWELVE, BUT YOU CAN'T FLY. YOU HAVEN'T TRAINED ENOUGH!
IT'S ALL BECAUSE YOU KEEP CLINGING TO SUIRO!
...THE THUNDER BEAST WILL BITE YOU AND KILL YOU.
...AND FLY OUT. IF YOU CANNOT ESCAPE QUICKLY
NOW GET IN THIS CAVE...
NOW FLY.
NOW.
...AND WAS STRUCK BY LIGHTNING.
I HEARD THE NEWS AND ENTERED THE CAVE TO RESCUE YOU ...
YOU COULD NOT FLY.

...
BROTHER SUIRO ...
BUT ...
...LOOK AT MY WINGS.
I CANNOT FLY ANY-MORE.
I LOST MY WINGS BECAUSE I RESCUED YOU ...
...SHINJURO!

YOU'VE GROWN UP, SHINJURO.
YOU CAN FLY THE SKIES NOW ...
...LIKE A PROPER TENGU.

I SHOULDN'T ...
...HAVE SPOKEN TO YOU THAT DAY.
PLEASE DON'T SAY THAT ...
...BROTHER SUIRO.

PLEASE ...
IF IT IS YOUR DESIRE...
...I WILL NOT FIGHT BACK.
OF ALL THOSE IN THIS MOUNTAIN ...
...I ...

...LOVED BROTHER SUIRO THE MOST ...
THE SOUND OF A FLUTE.
IT'S THE UZUZAKURA SONG ...
SO WHAT IF IT IS?!

FWOOSH
THAT MEANS YOU'RE NOT SUIRO.
...ON THE TOP OF THE MOUNTAIN.
...IS PLAYING MY FAVORITE SONG FOR ME ...
THE REAL SUIRO ...

Shinjuro.
Do not let the illusions of the fog trap you.
Do not get lost...
SHINJURO-SAMA!

HOW SHOULD I GREET YOU?

I AM ANXIOUS...

...BUT I'M NO LONGER...

...HESITANT TO GO FORWARD.

Kamisama Kiss
Chapter 53
THIS IS IT.
THIS IS THE TENGU VILLAGE OF KURAMA.

I SHOULDN'T BE SAYING THIS RIGHT AFTER WE'VE ARRIVED ...
THE FOG IS GONE BUT THE MIASMA IS STILL THICK.
...BUT ...
...I HAVE TO GO TO THE BATHROOM!
THAT'S CUZ WE'RE VERY CLOSE TO THE CLOUDS HERE.

Creak

WE SHOULDN'T BE TALKING HERE, SO LET'S GO IN!
Stomp
Stomp
W-WAIT NANAMI!
I'M NOT READY YET ...

WOW.

WELCOME HOME ...
...SHINJURO.

NOW, SHIN-JURO!
BROTHER SUIRO!
WOMP
I'M GLAD YOU'VE RETURNED SAFELY, BOTAN-MARU.
IT HAS BEEN A WHILE ...
...BROTHER SUIRO ...
KURAMA IS ALWAYS SO PROUD ...
...YET HE'S BOWING SO DEEPLY.

Pat
LET ME SEE YOUR FACE.
...
RAISE YOUR HEAD.
TMP
Rub
Rub
UM ...

Fwip
...
A hand-shake?
I'M NANAMI MOMO-ZONO, A TOCHIGAMI.
THAT'S TOMOE, MY SHINSHI.
I HOPE YOU DON'T MIND THAT WE CAME TOO.
OH?
YOUR COMPANIONS MUST BE TIRED FROM WALKING THE MOUNTAIN PATH.
YOU SHOULD ALL COME TO MY PLACE.
WHAT WAS THAT?
I GOTTA GO TO THE BATHROOM ...
BATH-ROOM.
THIS MOUNTAIN HAS BECOME A LONELY PLACE.
THE GRASS AND TREES DON'T GROW BECAUSE OF THE MIASMA.
AND THE ETERNAL CHERRY BLOSSOM TREE THAT WAS THE CENTER OF THE MOUNTAIN HAS FINALLY WITHERED.

...
YOU HAD TO LEAVE THE TRAINING HALL BECAUSE OF ME ...
BE-CAUSE I ...
IT IS DRAFTY, BUT I LIKE IT.
...BUT JIRO WON'T LET YOU IN.
I WANTED YOU TO BE ABLE TO RELAX IN THE WARM MAIN TRAINING HALL ...
So you'll stay here.
I ASSUMED YOU WERE LIVING SOMEWHERE IN THE TRAINING HALL.
WHY ARE YOU LIVING IN THIS OLD HOUSE, BROTHER SUIRO?
Fidget Fidget
UM, SUIRO.
UM ...
Rub Rub Rub
...I ...
WHA?!
Fwip
I SHALL SHOW HER THE WAY TO THE RESTROOM, THEN.
Smile
OH-HO, IS THAT SO, SHINSHI-DONO?
My, my.
SUIRO-DONO.
EXCUSE ME, BUT MY MASTER IS REALLY DYING TO GO TO THE BATHROOM.
She's been holding it all this time.

All right, Nanami?
I'LL ACCOMPANY HER.
...SO THE RESTROOM IS FAR AWAY. WILL SHE BE ABLE TO CONTROL HERSELF UNTIL THEN?
THIS IS A SHABBY PLACE ...
Y...
YOU DON'T NEED TO SHOW ME THE WAY!
I'll GO By myself!

THE MOTHER'S PROBABLY LOOKING FOR IT.
DAIDAIMARU, DON'T BRING IT HERE. YOU'LL GET SCOLDED!
THE MAMA BOAR WAS DEAD.
BABY WAS RIGHT BESIDE THE DEAD BODY.
A DEMON MUST HAVE KILLED HER.

THE MAIN TRAINING HALL.
BROTHER CHIYO-MARU.
I FOUND A BABY BOAR.

5

A lot of tengu appear in this volume, characters you're meeting for the first time! I'll be happy if you remember their names! ✿

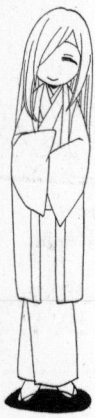

IF I LEAVE THE BABY ALONE, IT WILL BE KILLED TOO.

I FEEL SORRY FOR IT.

I WANNA TAKE CARE OF IT ...

...UNTIL SPRING, WHEN IT'S STRIPES ARE GONE.

...

ALL RIGHT, FINE.

BUT DON'T TELL THE BIG BROTHERS ABOUT IT.

OR THEY'LL THROW IT AWAY!

ALL RIGHT!

STAB
IF IT'S GONNA DIE IF YOU DON'T TAKE CARE OF IT ...
...IT WASN'T FATED TO LIVE LONG.
IF YOU CAN'T SURVIVE ON YOUR OWN ...
THE WEAK DIE OFF.
BECOME STRONG IF YOU DON'T WANT TO DIE.

...YOU'RE FATED TO DIE YOUNG TOO.
SH OVE
OOH, SCARY.
YOU LOOK LIKE YOU'RE ABOUT TO KILL SOMEONE TODAY ...
...JIRO-DONO.

YATORI.
THE ETERNAL CHERRY BLOSSOM... WHAT'S ITS NAME?
EVERYONE HERE IS SO GLOOMY NOW THAT THE TREE WITHERED.
THE ELDERS LAMENT OVER WHETHER THE MOUNTAIN IS FINISHED OR NOT.
Chomp
Chomp
Chomp
THEY'RE BEING SO RUDE, WHEN YOU'RE GOING TO BE THE FOURTH SOJOBO.
WHY DON'T YOU PLANT A NEW TREE?
IF YOU REPLACE THAT TREE YOURSELF ...
...EVERY-ONE WILL KNOW IT'S THE BEGIN-NING OF A NEW ERA!
Chomp
Chomp
Chomp

HOW ABOUT IT, JIRO-DONO?
Plop Plop
WHAM
YOU HAVE NO MANNERS!
HOW DARE YOU SNACK IN FRONT OF YOUR ELDER?!
THE ETERNAL CHERRY BLOSSOM TREE HAS BEEN THE MOUNTAIN'S SACRED TREE SINCE ANCIENT TIMES!
I WILL NOT ALLOW THAT RUDE MOUTH OF YOURS TO TELL ME TO GET RID OF IT.
How could you? Even Akura-oh-sama has never hit me.
BUT SHINJURO-DONO HAS RETURNED.
WHAT'RE YOU GOING TO DO IF THE OTHER TENGU SUGGEST MAKING HIM THE FOURTH SOJOBO?
YOU DON'T SEEM TOO POPULAR.
I AM THE STRONGEST TENGU ON THIS MOUNTAIN NOW ...
...SO I DESERVE TO BECOME THE FOURTH SOJOBO.

I CAN RUN FARTHER AND FLY HIGHER THAN ANYONE.
...SIMPLY BECAUSE I WANTED TO BECOME STRONG.
I MUST INHERIT THE THIRD SOJOBO'S POWERS ...
I SPENT MY DAYS IN TRAINING. I DID NOT ALLOW MYSELF TO BE LAZY.
...BEFORE HE DIES.
THE SUCCESSION RITE WILL BE HELD IN A FEW DAYS.
AT LAST.
I WON'T LET ANYBODY INTERFERE.
I TRAINED MYSELF ...

NOT SUIRO, NOT SHINJURO.
I SHALL BECOME THE STRONGEST TENGU OF ALL.
SHOOT.
Dash
THAT BATHROOM WAS UN-BELIEVABLY FAR AWAY!
It was like, a bus stop away.
IT WAS PRETTY CLEAN, SO THAT WAS GOOD...
I will not have you use my bath-room.
SUIRO DOESN'T SEEM TO LIKE ME.
DOES HE NOT TRUST ME?
Sniff Sniff

FWOOSH
YES.
MANY OF THE TREES ARE DEAD.
IT'S BECAUSE OF THE MIASMA.
THIS IS A BIG TREE... IS IT A CHERRY BLOSSOM TREE?
IT'S ROTTED AWAY ...
THE TENGU VILLAGE.

KICK
DON'T TOUCH IT, HUMAN!
OUCH!
WHAT'RE YOU DOING ?!
You guys are so cute! ♡
Wah, don't come over here!
Are you all kid tengu?
!
THIS IS THE ETERNAL CHERRY BLOSSOM TREE!
IF OUTSIDERS TOUCH IT, THEY'LL BE PUNISHED!
THE ETERNAL CHERRY BLOSSOM TREE?

SO IT IS A CHERRY BLOSSOM TREE.
IT'S ROTTING AWAY.
You gotta do something about it.
Wah, don't touch it!
THIS SACRED TREE STANDS IN THE CENTER OF THE MOUNTAIN.
IT BLOOMS EVERY FOUR YEARS ...
...AND THE FLOWERS ARE REALLY BEAUTIFUL.
This tree really is something.
Yeah, yeah.
!
Y...
YOU'VE GOT BOOBS ...
S-SHE'S ...
A WOMAN!
SHE'S A WOMAN!
BLANCH

YES ...
I AM.
I SPOKE WITH A FEMALE!
Waah!
WHY SHOULDN'T YOU TALK WITH ME?
You're being rude.
THE BIG BROTHERS WILL SCOLD ME!
WE SHOULD NOT LOOK AT A FEMALE, NOR TALK TO ONE.
WE'LL FALL INTO THE HUMAN WORLD IF WE TOUCH A PRETTY YOUNG FEMALE ...
Pretty...
First time someone's called me that.
I...
Heh, Heh,
Sorry! I talked to you.
I'M NOT THAT PRETTY ...
HMM, HOLD IT.

THEN WE SHOULD BE ALL RIGHT.
We can talk to her.
BROTHER SUIRO IS MUCH PRETTIER.
IS SHE PRETTY?
Well, she's young.
BROTHER.
BROTHER.
I'D LIKE TO DIG A HOLE BY THE ETERNAL CHERRY BLOSSOM TREE ...
...AND BURY THIS BABY BOAR THERE.
DEMONS STARTED ROAMING THE MOUNTAIN, AND THERE'RE FEWER ANIMALS NOW.
AFTER SOJOBO-SAMA COLLAPSED, THE CLOUDS OF MIASMA SHOWED UP.

YOU'LL BE FINE.
SOJOBO-SAMA WILL RECOVER SOON ...
...AND THE MOUNTAIN WILL BE BACK TO NORMAL!
THE ETERNAL CHERRY BLOSSOM TREE HAS WITHERED TOO.
I WONDER WHAT'S GONNA HAPPEN TO THIS VILLAGE.
YOU SURE ?!
YEAH.
SHE'S LYING. BROTHER JIRO SAID SOJOBO-SAMA WILL DIE SOON.
THAT'S WHY BROTHER JIRO IS GONNA BECOME THE FOURTH SOJOBO.
BUT WILL THE MOUN-TAIN BE BACK TO NORMAL ...
...AFTER JIRO BECOMES THE FOURTH SOJOBO?
WILL THIS ETERNAL CHERRY BLOSSOM TREE ...
...BLOOM AGAIN?

Squeeze
I CAN'T GET RID OF THE CLOUDS OF MIASMA COVERING THIS MOUNTAIN...
...BUT ...
SO PLEASE ...
...I WANT TO MAKE THE CLOUDS IN THEIR HEARTS DISAPPEAR.

BLOOM, CHERRY BLOSSOM TREE...

YOU WERE RIGHT.
IT BLOOMED
THE FLOWERS ARE BEAUTIFUL.
I'M GLAD I WAS ABLE TO SEE THEM BLOOM.
ARE WE DREAMING?
THE FLOWERS OF THE ETERNAL CHERRY BLOSSOM TREE!

BING BONG
IT'S THE EVENING BELL.
WE GOTTA RETURN TO THE TRAINING HALL ...
...AND PRE-PARE DINNER.
All right.
WE'LL TELL EVERYONE ABOUT THE ETERNAL CHERRY BLOSSOM TREE
SAY.
DID YOU ...
...MAYBE... COME DOWN TO THIS MOUNTAIN ...
...TO HELP US?
ARE YOU A MAIDEN FROM THE SKIES?

NOW, GO HOME QUICK.
YOU'RE JUST A KID. DON'T SAY SUCH THINGS.
WHAP
THANK YOU, SISTER.
I'M...
...SO GLAD...
FWOOSH
WHA?

THE FLOWERS ...
...ARE SCATTERING!
SO...
...MY POWERS CAN'T KEEP IT BLOOMING...
...QUICKLY ...
WE MUST...
...HELP SOJOBO-SAN RECOVER QUICKLY....
RUSTLE

Deep in the mountains.

In the Kurama village where females are forbidden entry...
...a man met a maiden from the skies.

Kamisama Kiss
Chapter 54

IS SHE A MAIDEN FROM THE SKIES?
UMM ...
HE'S AN ADULT TENGU ...
UM.
Oh!

WHO ARE YOU?
THIS IS A SACRED MOUNTAIN WHERE FEMALES ARE FORBIDDEN TO ENTER.
WHO GAVE YOU PERMISSION TO COME TO THIS MOUNTAIN?
FEMALES ARE FORBIDDEN TO ENTER HERE?!
THAT'S WHY...
...HE'S SO ANGRY ...
I...
I'M SORRY.
I DIDN'T MEAN TO ...
LIE
Fwip
I'LL LEAVE THE MOUNTAIN NOW!
GRAB
WAIT.
DID YOU MAKE THIS TREE BLOOM?

WHY DID YOU COME HERE?
WHAT IS YOUR NAME?
YOU'RE HURTING ME.
I'LL BREAK YOUR ARM IF YOU DO NOT ANSWER.
WHA...?

JIRO-SAMA.
MMM.
JIRO ?!
HE'S THE JERK WHO HURT BOTANMARU!
Bite
STOVE

JIRO-SAMA.
THERE YOU ARE.
PLEASE RETURN TO THE TRAINING HALL ...

IS SOME-THING WRONG ?

WAIT!
...

A WOMAN'S ARM ...
...IS AWFULLY THIN ...
WHAT WAS THAT ?!
HE WAS SUCH A SAVAGE TENGU!
SOMEONE LIKE HIM BECOMING THE FOURTH SOJOBO ...
BUT WILL THE MOUNTAIN BE BACK TO NORMAL?
OF COURSE IT WON'T!
Slip
YAH!

SPLAT
YOU WERE GONE FOR A LONG TIME.
WHERE WERE YOU WANDERING?
TOMOE.

SOME-THING WRONG?
YOU'RE SHAKING. WHAT HAPPENED?
I'M...
...SHAK-ING?
I'M...

...GLAD I WAS ABLE TO GET AWAY ...
YOU MET JIRO?!
I HOPE YOU WEREN'T HURT.
UH...
Fuss Fuss
I MET HIM.
HE ONLY GRABBED MY ARM ...
I DIDN'T KNOW FEMALES WERE FORBIDDEN TO ENTER THE MOUNTAIN.
I WAS WANDERING AROUND.
The bathroom was so far away.
I'M GLAD NOTHING HAPPENED.
Relieved
I'M OVER HERE!

I'VE HEARD ABOUT THIS JIRO, BUT HE ...
...IS REALLY SAVAGE.
HE HAS ALWAYS BEEN COARSE AND CLUMSY.
I SHOULD'VE BEEN MORE CAREFUL.
I WILL PREPARE ANOTHER BATH-ROOM.
Argh!
I'M GETTING REALLY ANNOYED, SUIRO!
WHY WON'T YOU LOOK AT ME?!
I'LL FORCE YOU TO LOOK ME IN THE EYE WHILE YOU'RE SPEAK-ING TO ME!
GRAB

!
EX-CUSE ME ...
Fwip

I HAVE BEEN LIVING HERE FOR A LONG TIME ...
...SO I AM NOT ACCUS-TOMED TO DEALING WITH FEMALES.

SO THAT'S WHY YOU DIDN'T LET ME USE YOUR BATH-ROOM?
I THOUGHT A WOMAN WOULD PREFER A FLUSH TOILET.
The amenities here are not modern.

HAVING HIM SAY THAT DOESN'T MAKE ME HAPPY AT ALL ...
Grr
You're pretty.
ESPECIALLY A BEAUTIFUL GIRL LIKE YOU ...

BROTHER SUIRO ...
I'm done with my meal.
WHY DON'T WE TALK ABOUT THE MOUNTAIN?
It's about time

THAT WAS JUST WHEN I WAS A KID ...
LET'S TALK ABOUT MY FATHER'S ILLNESS.

OHO, YOU'VE EATEN ALL THE PICKLES, SHINJURO.
!
Ah.
THESE PICKLES ARE GOOD.
YOU CAN EAT VINEGAR PICKLES NOW?

NANAMI GOT THIS MEDICINE IN IZUMO FROM A HEALER KAMI.
FATHER MIGHT RECOVER IF HE TAKES THIS.
Tmp
IT'S MOMOTAN.

LET'S GIVE IT TO HIM.
THE MOUNTAIN WILL BE BACK TO NORMAL WHEN HE RECOVERS!
THEN JIRO DOESN'T NEED TO SUCCEED HIM.
IF THIS IS REALLY MOMOTAN ...
First time I've seen it.
...IT MIGHT WORK FOR SOJOBO ...
HOW-EVER.
WE WON'T BE ABLE TO DELIVER IT TO HIM.

SOJOBO COLLAPSED ABOUT TWO MONTHS AGO.
SINCE THEN, HE'S SOMEWHERE IN THE TRAINING HALL, BUT I DON'T KNOW WHERE.
JIRO IS IN CHARGE OF OFFICIAL AFFAIRS, AND THE TRAINING HALL IS HEAVILY GUARDED.
OUT-SIDERS CANNOT ENTER THE TRAINING HALL.
SHK SHK
WHICH BOTH YOU AND I ARE.
WE COULD GIVE THE MEDICINE TO SOME-ONE INSIDE ...
...BUT IT WOULD NOT REACH SOJOBO.
JIRO WOULD TAKE IT AWAY.
I IMAGINE SO...

DON'T TORTURE YOURSELF, SHINJURO.
EAT SOME APPLES.
THINGS WILL COME OUT RIGHT, SOME-HOW.
THEN YOU'RE NOT GONNA DO ANYTHING ?!
NO, THAT WOULD BE DANGER-OUS.
BROTHER SUIRO!
I CANNOT ALLOW YOU TO DO SUCH A THING.
I'LL GO TALK TO JIRO!
I'LL GO SEE FATHER IN PERSON!
I'M NOT A CHILD ANY-MORE.
I CAME HERE CUZ I THOUGHT I COULD DO SOMETHING TOO.
I'M NOT THE KID I USED TO BE!

KURAMA...
...
NO.
YOU AREN'T ABLE TO DO ANYTHING YET.
WH...

BANG
SHIN-JURO!
WHY NOT ...
I AM SO GLAD YOU'VE RETURNED!
I'VE BEEN WAITING FOR YOU TO COME HOME EVERY DAY THESE PAST TWO MONTHS!
OOH! YOU'VE GROWN UP SO!
I KNEW YOU'D BECOME A FINE TENGU!
GRAB
Um.
WHO ARE YOU?

MOB
MOB
I TOLD HIM THAT SHINJURO-SAMA HAS RETURNED.
MOVE OVER, BOTAN-MARU.
AH.
IT'S ME!
The Tutor
...
WHA ...?
SHINJURO HAS RETURNED TO BECOME THE FOURTH SOJOBO!
ISN'T THAT SO, SHIN-JURO?!

WE NEED TO CHOOSE HIS SUCCESSOR.
EVEN IF HE SURVIVES THIS TIME, WHO KNOWS WHAT'LL HAPPEN AFTER THAT?
SOJOBO IS OLD.
I brought some good medicine
HOLD IT, WHO'S SAYING THAT?
I CAME HERE TO GET FATHER BETTER ...
SHIN-JURO.
EVERYTHING IS FOR THE SAKE OF THIS MOUNTAIN.
WE CANNOT AFFORD TO MAKE JIRO THE FOURTH SOJOBO.
NO.
YOU WILL NOT REFUSE.

6

This is the last sidebar. Thank you for reading this far.

Thank you for your letters. They always cheer me up.

If you have any comments about this volume, please send your letters to the following address...

P.O. Box 11010
San Francisco, CA
94101

Please

Thank you.

Then!

I pray from my heart that we'll be able to meet again in volume 10 as well.

-Julietta Suzuki

COME, COME, ELDERS.
Clap Clap
SHINJURO IS STILL TIRED FROM HIS TRIP.
LET US TALK ABOUT THIS LATER.
MMM ...
YOU'RE RIGHT.
SHIN-JURO ...
YOU DO NOT NEED TO WORRY OVER THIS MATTER.
STOMP
SHIN-JURO?

SORRY, BROTHER SUIRO.
I'LL GO COOL MY HEAD A LITTLE.
Bang
WILL KURAMA BE ALL RIGHT?
HE DOESN'T WANT TO BECOME THE FOURTH SOJOBO.
I CAN UNDERSTAND. HE'S BEEN LIVING IN THE HUMAN WORLD FOR 17 YEARS NOW.
TOCHI-GAMI-DONO.
I'LL ACCEPT A LITTLE OF THIS MOMOTAN FOR SOJOBO ...
...BUT YOU TWO TAKE SHINJURO AND LEAVE THIS MOUN-TAIN EARLY TOMORROW MORNING ...
...BEFORE YOU GET INVOLVED IN OUR TROUBLES.

I DON'T MIND TROUBLE.
WE CAME HERE TO ASSIST KURA-SHINJURO ...
...SO WE'RE NOT GOING TO LEAVE UNTIL HE DOES.
WHEN I MET SHINJURO AT THE MAIN GATE ...
..I REALIZED HE WAS NO LONGER THE CHILD I USED TO KNOW ...
...BECAUSE HE WAS WITH YOU.
HIS BODY IS NOT SOLELY OF THIS MOUNTAIN ANYMORE.
HE MUST HAVE LOTS OF THINGS IN THE HUMAN WORLD THAT HE CANNOT ABANDON.

DO YOU KNOW WHAT SHINJURO IS REALLY LIKE, TOCHI-GAMI-DONO?
HUH ?
...WILL NOT ASK HIM TO BECOME PART OF THIS MOUNTAIN AGAIN.
I...
HE DOES NOT KNOW HOW TO ASK OTHERS FOR HELP.
HE TRIES TO DO EVERY-THING ALONE, EVEN WHEN HE CAN'T HANDLE IT HIMSELF.
HE SHOULDERS EVERYTHING ALONE.
SO I HAVE ALWAYS QUIETLY WATCHED OVER HIM ...
...SO HE NEED NOT SHOULDER MORE BURDENS.
HE HAS NEVER ASKED ME TO HELP HIM ...
...EVEN THOUGH WE'VE BEEN TOGETHER SINCE HE WAS A CHILD.

FWOOSH
PLEASE TAKE HIM HOME ...
...BEFORE HE AGREES TO BECOME THE FOURTH SOJOBO.
YOU CAN'T DO IT.
YOU'RE NOT GONNA BE ABLE TO SNEAK INTO THAT TRAINING HALL ALONE.
YOU DIDN'T EVEN REALIZE I WAS HERE UNTIL I RAISED MY VOICE.

I CAN FEEL THE PRESSURE OF THE TRAINING HALL EVEN AT THIS DISTANCE.
TWO, THREE SHIELDS HAVE BEEN SET UP AROUND IT.
BROTHER SUIRO MUST'VE TOLD YOU TO LEAVE.
OH?
I WAS THINKING THE SAME THING.
I TALKED BIG, BUT I WASN'T REALLY READY TO DO ANYTHING.
I SUCK SO MUCH, I WANNA DIE.
BROTHER SUIRO SAW THROUGH THAT TOO.

SO.
WHAT DO YOU ...
...WANT TO DO?
KU-RAMA!
DASH
SLAM
Gah!
SO!
PANT
PANT
WHAT SHOULD WE DO NEXT?

I WANT TO SNEAK INTO THE TRAINING HALL ...
...AND GIVE FATHER HIS MEDICINE.
...
PLEASE ...
...LEND ME A HAND.

WHA? LEND YOU WHAT?
THE WIND'S STRONG AND I COULDN'T HEAR YOU. SAY IT ONE MORE TIME!
HEY TOMOE, WHAT DID HE SAY? WHAT DID HE SAY?!
SHUT UP! I DIDN'T SAY ANY-THING!
TO PLEASE LEND HIM A HAND.
WHAT THE HECK ?!
OF COURSE WE WILL.

The Otherworld

Ayakashi **is an archaic term for yokai.**

Kami **are Shinto deities or spirits. The word can be used for a range of creatures, from nature spirits to strong and dangerous gods.**

Kamuhakari **is the weeklong convocation of kami at Izumo Oyashiro shrine in October of the lunar calendar. Therefore in the lunar calendar, October is called Kamiarizuki (month-with-kami) in Izumo, and Kannazuki (month-without-kami) in other regions. Festivals are held at Izumo Oyashiro during the Kamuhakari.**

Onibi-warashi **are like will-o'-the-wisps.**

Shikigami **are spirits that are summoned and employed by** ***onmyoji*** **(Yin-Yang sorcerers).**

Shinshi **are birds, beasts, insects or fish that have a special relationship with a kami.**

Tochigami **(or** ***jinushigami*****) are deities of a specific area of land.**

Tsuriki **is a kami's power and becomes stronger the more it is used.**

Honorifics

-chan **is a diminutive most often used with babies, children or teenage girls.**

-dono **roughly means "my lord," although not in the aristocratic sense.**

-hime **means princess, although a Japanese princess is not the same as a Western one and isn't necessarily the daughter of a king.**

-san **is a standard honorific similar to Mr., Mrs., Miss, or Ms.**

-sama **is used with people of much higher rank.**

Notes

Page 23, panel 5: Ikebana
Traditional Japanese flower arranging.

Page 40, panel 2: Waratte Iikamo
Spoofing a Japanese TV show called *Waratte Iitomo* that is broadcast at noon on weekdays.

Page 41, panel 1: Go-kon
A group dating event where the same number of males and females gather for activities like karaoke.

Page 79, panel 1: Mount Takao
A mountain about an hour away from Tokyo where, according to folklore, tengu live.

Page 104, panel 2: Futon
Traditional Japanese bedding. Japanese futon are much lighter than Western ones, and are designed to be folded and stored during the day.

Page 104, panel 3: Tatami
Straw mats that make up traditional Japanese flooring.

Page 111, panel 1: Sojogadani Valley
An actual valley northwest of Mount Kurama.

Page 111, panel 2: Negative ions
Negatively charged ions are released by bodies of water and green areas such as forests. Negative ions are said to have health benefits, including making you feel energized and invigorated.

Page 114, panel 4: Atago, Takao
One of the eight great tengu (*hachi daitengu*) is said to live on Mount Atago. Another of the eight great tengu, Naigubu, is said to live on Mount Takao.

Page 115, panel 2: Uzuzakura
Cherry blossoms that bloom on Mount Kurama.

Julietta Suzuki's debut manga *Hoshi ni Naru Hi* (The Day One Becomes a Star) appeared in the 2004 *Hana to Yume Plus*. Her other books include *Akuma to Dolce* (The Devil and Sweets) and *Karakuri Odette*. Born in December in Fukuoka Prefecture, she enjoys having movies play in the background while she works on her manga.

KAMISAMA KISS
VOL. 9
Shojo Beat Edition

STORY AND ART BY
Julietta Suzuki

English Translation & Adaptation/Tomo Kimura
Touch-up Art & Lettering/Joanna Estep
Design/Yukiko Whitley
Editor/Pancha Diaz

KAMISAMA HAJIMEMASHITA by Julietta Suzuki
© Julietta Suzuki 2011
All rights reserved.
First published in Japan in 2011 by HAKUSENSHA, Inc., Tokyo.
English language translation rights arranged with
HAKUSENSHA, Inc., Tokyo.

The stories, characters and incidents mentioned
in this publication are entirely fictional.

No portion of this book may be reproduced or transmitted
in any form or by any means without written permission
from the copyright holders.

Printed in Canada

Published by VIZ Media, LLC
P.O. Box 77010
San Francisco, CA 94107

10 9 8 7 6 5 4 3 2 1
First printing, June 2012

www.viz.com

www.shojobeat.com

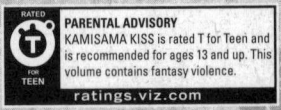

Skip·Beat!★™

By Yoshiki Nakamura

Kyoko Mogami followed her true love Sho to Tokyo to support him while he made it big as an idol. But he's casting her out now that he's famous! Kyoko won't suffer in silence—she's going to get her sweet revenge by beating Sho in show biz!

Shojo Beat™
MANGA from the HEART

Only $8.99

On sale at:
www.shojobeat.com

Also available at your local bookstore and comic store.

Skip·Beat! © Yoshiki Nakamura 2002/HAKUSENSHA, Inc.

Can love trump a cursed life?

Sawako's a shy, lonely, pure-hearted student who just happens to look like the scary girl in a famous horror movie! But when she manages to befriend the most popular boy in school, will her frightful reputation scare off her best chance for love?

kimi ni todoke

From Me to You

By Karuho Shiina

Find out in the *Kimi ni Todoke* manga—
BUY YOURS TODAY!

Winner of the 2008 Kodansha Manga Award
(shojo category)

On sale at **www.shojobeat.com**
Also available at your local bookstore or comic store.

KIMI NI TODOKE © 2005 Karuho Shiina/SHUEISHA Inc.

love★com

By Aya Nakahara

Class clowns Risa and Ôtani join forces to find love!

Manga available now

Shojo Beat

On sale at www.shojobeat.com
Also available at your local bookstore and comic store

LOVE★COM © 2001 by Aya Nakahara/SHUEISHA Inc.

RATED T TEEN ratings.viz.com

viz media
www.viz.com

High School DEBUT

By Kazune Kawahara

When Haruna Nagashima was in junior high, softball and comics were her life. Now that she's in high school, she's ready to find a boyfriend. But will hard work (and the right coach) be enough?

Find out in the *High School Debut* manga series—available now!

On sale at:
www.shojobeat.com

Also available at your local bookstore and comic store.

ratings.viz.com

KOKO DEBUT © 2003 by Kazune Kawahara/SHUEISHA Inc.

The VIZ Manga App has some new friends...

The world's best manga is now on the iPad,™ iPhone™ and iPod touch™

To learn more, visit viz.com/25years

From legendary manga like *Death Note* to *Absolute Boyfriend*, the best manga in the world is now available on multiple devices through the official VIZ Manga app.

- Hundreds of volumes available
- Free App
- New content weekly
- Free chapter 1 previews

HEROES OF MANGA
viz.com/25years

ZETTAI KARESHI © 2003 Yuu WATASE/Shogakukan, KEKKAISHI © 2004 Yellow TANABE/Shogakukan, Vampire Knight © Matsuri Hino 2004/HAKUSENSHA, Inc., BLACK BIRD © 2007 Kanoko SAKURAKOUJI/Shogakukan, BAKUMAN。© 2008 by Tsugumi Ohba, Takeshi Obata/SHUEISHA Inc. ONE PIECE © 1997 by Eiichiro Oda/SHUEISHA Inc., BLEACH © 2001 by Tite Kubo/SHUEISHA Inc. NARUTO © 1999 by Masashi Kishimoto/SHUEISHA Inc. DEATH NOTE © 2003 by Tsugumi Ohba, Takeshi Obata/SHUEISHA Inc.

This is the last page.

In keeping with the original Japanese comic format, this book reads from right to left—so action, sound effects, and word balloons are completely reversed. This preserves the orientation of the original artwork—plus, it's fun! Check out the diagram shown here to get the hang of things, and then turn to the other side of the book to get started!